BENJAMIN BRIT

Two Lullabies for
Two Pianos

(1936)

FABER MUSIC

© 1990 by Faber Music Ltd
First published in 1990 by Faber Music Ltd
3 Queen Square London WC1N 3AU
Music drawn by Sambo Music Engraving Co
Cover design by M & S Tucker
Printed in England

Duration: 3 minutes each

Even for such a hard-working and prolific composer as Britten, 1936 was an exceptionally busy year, and it is remarkable that he found time to attempt to establish a two-piano partnership with the South African-born pianist and composer, Adolph Hallis (1896–1987), in the early months of that year. The two of them were offered a BBC audition on 19 March, and Britten's diary records that on 10 March, in London, he began work on 'a Lullaby for 2 pianos – not very good or typical I'm afraid', completing and copying it out the next day, when the two pianists had a rehearsal. Though Britten's self-deprecating remarks are not at all unusual, his entry for Saturday 14 March (at his mother's house in Frinton) unexpectedly reads 'peace of mind is disturbed by thought that before I go back I have to write a Lullaby stunt for Adolph H & me to play at BBC on Thursday. My brain so far is an utter blank.' The next day '. . . have to force myself to sit down & write a Lullaby for a Retired Colonel for Adolph . . . I concoct something – & surprisingly effective too'. This second Lullaby (the significance of whose title is not clear, although the musical quotations are self-explanatory) was finished and copied on the following day, and after several rehearsals the audition took place 'in [the BBC] concert hall, with vile pianos, & gloomy atmosphere. We play 3 pieces & depart in silence.'

While we may disagree with Britten's estimation of the first Lullaby, it is safe to assume that it was not played at the audition; and that the evidently unhappy circumstances of the first performance of the second one put any thoughts of a future, either for the piece or for the duo, out of Britten's mind.'* The whereabouts of the copies that were needed for the audition is not known. Britten calls them '1st piano part' in his diary, implying that he played the second piano, no doubt using the pencil composition sketches (now in the Britten-Pears Library at Aldeburgh). These are both marked with a number of corrections in ink, so it may be taken for granted that, in spite of the absence of the copies, the reading of the surviving manuscripts is accurate. As usual with Britten, only minor editorial adjustments were needed for this first publication.

The *Two Lullabies* were heard in public for the first time at the 40th Aldeburgh Festival, on 22 June 1988 in Snape Maltings, when the pianists were Peter Frankl and Tamás Vásáry.

C.M.

*But in December 1936 Adolph Hallis was the pianist in the first performance of Britten's *Temporal Variations* (another work that was put aside after its first performance), and Britten remained in touch with him at least until 1939.

Lullaby

BENJAMIN BRITTEN
(1913–1976)

[March 10th-11th 1936]

Lullaby for a Retired Colonel

* The Ms. has E♭, not F here, and on the first beat of the following bar.

March 15th-16th 1936